Fiction Teacher's Book 2
Wendy Body

Series Editor: Wendy Body

Pearson Education Limited
Edinburgh Gate
Harlow
Essex
CM20 2JE
England and Associated Companies throughout the World

ISBN 0582 50395 7
First published 2001

Printed in Great Britain by Scotprint, Haddington
Designed by AMR, Bramley, Hants

The Publisher's policy is to use paper manufactured from sustainable forests.

Edinburgh Gate
Harlow, Essex

If you wish to enlarge any of the Shared Writing Examples for use in your teaching, you may do so.

Remember that the commentary you give while you are writing is crucial for children's learning, so routinely comment on:

- the spelling of more difficult words

- the sentence punctuation

- why you have chosen certain words

- how you can change your mind and alter things while writing.

Contents

Year 2 Fiction Summary Chart

Text in Resource Book	Text level Objective	Sentence level Objective Links	Unit of work
Term 1 Unit 1 Money Doesn't Grow On Trees	**T9**: to apply phonological, graphic knowledge andsight vocabulary to spell words accurately	**S3**: to ... take account of commas and exclamation marks in reading aloud ...	Learn selected spellings
Term 1 Unit 2 Money Doesn't Grow On Trees	**T10**: to use story structure to write about own experience	**S5**: to revise knowledge about other uses of capitalisation e.g. for names ... emphasis	Plan a story
Term 1 Unit 3 Jonah's Den	**T11**: to use language of time... to structure a sequence of events	**S2**: to find examples ... of words and phrases that link sentences ...	Structure events in a story
Term 1 Unit 4 Jonah's Den	**T10**: to use story structure to write about own experience ...	**S4**: to re-read own writing for sense and punctuation	Write a similar story
Term 1 Unit 5 Five fat sausages	**T12**: to use simple poetry structures and to substitute own ideas		Write rhymes base based on the model
Term 1 Unit 6 Fishes in the sea!	**T12**: use simple poetry structures and ... write new lines		Continue the poem
Term 2 Unit 7 First extract from Little Red Riding Hood	**T12**: to apply phonological, graphic knowledge and sight vocabulary to spell words accurately		Find the missing words and spell them
Term 2 Unit 8 Second extract from Little Red Riding Hood	**T14**: to write character profiles eg simple descriptions ... using key words and phrases that describe ... characters in the text	**S9**: to secure the use of simple sentences in own writing	Write a character profile
Term 2 Unit 9 A Magical Cave	**T13**: to use story settings from reading eg re-describe, use in own writing	**S3**: to re-read own writing to check for grammatical sense (coherence) and accuracy (agreement)	Describe the setting for a story
Term 2 Unit 10 A Magical Cave	**T13**: to use story settings from reading e.g. ... write a different story in the same setting	**S5**: to use verb tenses with increasing accuracy e.g. ... see/saw, go/went and to use past tense consistently ...	Write a story

Term 2 Unit 11 The Inside–Outside Man	**T15**: to use structures from poems as a basis for writing, by extending or substituting elements		Add verses to a poem
Term 2 Unit 12 The Inside–Outside Man	**T14**: to write character profiles, e.g. simple descriptions ... using key words and phrases that describe ... characters in the text	**S3**: to re-read own writing to check for grammatical sense (coherence) and accuracy (agreement)	Write character descriptions
Term 2 Unit 13 The Inside–Outside Man	**T15**: to write own poems from initial jottings and words		Write a poem
Term 3 Unit 14 Strange Bumps	**T9**: to apply phonological, graphic knowledge and sight vocabulary to spell words accurately	**S2**: the need for grammatical agreement, matching verbs to nouns/pronouns	Write a story with correct spellings
Term 3 Unit 15 Writing Tongue Twisters	**T11**: to write tongue twisters or alliterative sentences	**S4**: to use commas in lists	Write tongue twisters
Term 3 Unit 16 Planning a Story	**T10**: to write sustained stories using knowledge of story elements: narrative, settings, characterisation, dialogue and the language of story		Plan a story
Term 3 Unit 17 Two Funny Limericks	**T11**: to use humorous verse as a structure ... to write their own by adaptation, mimicry or substitution	**S2**: the need for grammatical agreement, matching verbs to nouns/pronouns	Write limericks
Term 3 Unit 18 What will happen next? Lion at School	**T10**: to write sustained stories, using their knowledge of story elements: narrative, settings, characterisation, dialogue and the language of story	**S3**: to use standard forms of verbs ... and to use the past tense consistently for narration	Plan and continue the story
Term 3 Unit 19 Writing About A Book	**T12**: to write simple evaluations of books	**S5**: to write in clear sentences using capital letters and full stops accurately	Write a book review
Term 3 Unit 20 Riddle	**T11**: to invent own riddles, language puzzles, jokes		Write a riddle

Introduction

What Is Pelican Shared Writing?

Pelican Shared Writing is an easy-to-use resource for teaching shared writing. It comprises ten packs: one Fiction and one Non-Fiction for each year group for Years 2, 3, 4, 5 and 6. Per year group, it comprises:
- one Writing Resource Book
- one Teacher's Book with copymasters
- a large sheet of acetate and a Pelican Page Clip
- one CD-ROM of writing activities differentiated at three levels for use on screen or to print as worksheets.

Each Writing Resource Book offers 20 units of work which cover all the NLS Writing Composition objectives for the year group. Each Writing Composition objective forms one unit of work. Links are also made to appropriate Sentence Level objectives.

Although *Pelican Shared Writing* stands alone, it has links to *Pelican Guided Reading and Writing* in terms of objectives and tasks and there are content links to *Pelican Big Books*.

The Writing Resource Books

- Each 48-page big book is split into three parts – one for each term's teaching objectives.
- Shared writing is rooted in shared reading, and so the Writing Resource Books contain the texts which not only provide the starting point for writing, but also act as models of the genre to be studied. Story plans and writing frames are sometimes included as well.
- Quotes on and about the writing process from professional children's writers feature on the inside back cover of each Fiction Writing Resource Book to initiate discussions on writing.
- Each book comes with a large sheet of acetate and a Pelican Page Clip for text marking and writing.

The Teacher's Books

The Teacher's Book in each pack contains:
- teaching pages for each Unit of work with detailed, step-by-step advice on what to do for each shared writing session. There are also examples of completed activities which teachers can use to guide the class in composing a text. Units may take more than one shared writing session to complete in Years 3 to 6. Year 2 units are always split into two sessions.
- a small number of copymasters eg writing frames, character planners. These are for general use and can also be applied to other texts and writing activities.
- copymaster versions of all the Writing Resource Book texts. These can be used to make overhead transparencies and in instances where it is helpful for children to have their own copy of a text, e.g. for annotation.
- the Non-Fiction Teacher's Books have a summary of links to other areas of the curriculum on the inside back covers.

Teaching Shared Writing

Pelican Shared Writing complements the National Literacy Strategy's *Grammar for Writing*. *Pelican Shared Writing* concentrates on delivering the text level writing composition objectives whereas *Grammar for Writing* concentrates on sentence level objectives. *Pelican Shared Writing* adopts a similar approach to shared writing which may be summarised as follows:

Key Features of Shared Writing:

- Make explicit how purpose and audience determine form and style.
- Link the writing to specific objectives.
- Rehearse sentences orally before writing.
- Discuss and explain alternatives and choices.
- Keep rereading to maintain flow, meaning and consistency.
- Involve children in the revision and editing.

Shared Writing Techniques:

Teacher Demonstration

The teacher composes and writes, modelling for children how to compose a particular text type or tackle a writing activity. He/she thinks aloud, rehearses choices before writing, explains choices and makes changes. The children do not contribute to the composition but they are invited to offer opinions on, for example, the choice of words or sentence construction. Demonstration time will vary according to the nature of the text and children's competence.

Teacher Scribing

The teacher acts as scribe and builds on the initial demonstration by getting the children to make contributions to the composition or task. The teacher guides, focuses, explains and challenges the contributions e.g. *Why did you choose that word? That's a really good sentence because ...* . While children could make their contributions orally by putting up their hands, it is preferable for them to use whiteboards (in pairs or individually) which ensures participation by all children. It is also advisable to take "Time Out" i.e. get children to turn to each other in pairs and discuss possibilities for 30 seconds or so.

Supported Composition

Supported composition is preparation for independent writing. Children compose a limited amount of text using whiteboards or notebooks – in pairs or individually. Their alternatives are reviewed and discussed and choices and changes made. Some differentiation can be achieved by seating children in their ability groups and asking one group to orally compose one sentence, another to write one or two sentences and a third to write several sentences. Supported composition will enable you to identify those children who will need to repeat or continue the task in guided writing i.e. those who need greater support.

Shared writing is the most powerful means of improving and developing children's writing skills. But they will not develop into proficient writers unless firstly they are given sufficient TIME to practise the skills and craft of writing for themselves, and secondly, they receive the FEEDBACK which will help them evaluate what they have done and so learn from it.

Note: A Pelican Shared Writing CD-ROM is available for use alongside each year's work. For further details, please see the section on ICT, overleaf.

Teaching a Pelican Shared Writing Unit of work

Support for each step will be found on the teaching pages

Discussing the Text for each unit

- Introduce the task and the objective
- Read the text in the Resource Book with the class and discuss the content
- Draw out features of the genre.

Shared Writing

Using the Shared Writing Example and the teaching notes for guidance:

- Demonstrate or model the particular features of the writing
- Scribe and guide the pupils' contributions
- Continue with supported composition by children working in pairs
- Check the children's learning.

Independent Writing

- Children complete the writing task.
- They consolidate their learning by carrying out a suggested similar task.

Checking the Objective

- Determine children's understanding of the objective and how far they can apply their knowledge by evaluating their writing.

Revisiting the Objective

- If needs be, repeat the whole process using the suggested activity.

ICT and Pelican Shared Writing

ICT may be used by all pupils to support writing skills. The word processor or desktop publishing package can enable the child to focus on the development of ideas and the manipulation of the written word without the physical constraints imposed by the handwriting process. The ease of editing, the spell-checking facilities and the ability to move text around the page make ICT support programs valuable tools to include within the writing repertoire. Writing tasks offer the ideal opportunity to integrate and apply those ICT skills being developed in the ICT curriculum.

Almost any writing task may be approached using ICT as an optional writing tool. These writing tasks will offer strong links with the ICT curriculum, which aims for pupils to:

- 'develop their ability to apply their IT capability and ICT to support their use of language and communication'
- 'pass on ideas by communicating, presenting and exchanging information'
- 'develop language skills eg in systematic writing and in presenting their own ideas'
- 'be creative and persistent'
- 'recognise the strengths and limitations of ICT'

(QCA Scheme of Work for ICT, Aims and Purposes)

The 'Communicating' strand for ICT is inextricably linked with developing literacy. Computer access is a great resource for independent, group and class work, and is too valuable a tool to remain unused during the development of literacy skills. It is a great motivator and encourages collaborative work that can become more focused as children's attention is extended.

Within the suggested Year 2 Fiction Pelican Shared Writing activities, there are some clear links with Units from the QCA Scheme of Work for ICT, particularly Unit 2A: Writing Stories – Communicating information using text. Links to the most relevant National Curriculum Programme of Study for ICT are listed in the table opposite.

The differentiated writing frames for Year 2 (Fiction and Non-Fiction) are available on the CD-ROM entitled Pelican Shared Writing Year 2 (ISBN 0582 50985 8), which can be easily installed on any machine supporting Microsoft Word. Here they may be adapted, should you so wish, to suit your particular needs. The CD-ROM also provides cross-referencing charts for both Writing and ICT targets, including the ICT Programme of Study references and links to the QCA Scheme of Work for ICT – collated and readily available for inclusion into planning records.

Year 2 Fiction
Relevant objectives from the ICT Programme of Study

Pupils should be taught:

1a
to gather information from a variety of sources *[for example, people, books, databases, CD-ROMs, videos and TV]*

2a
to use text, tables, images and sound to develop their ideas

3a
how to share their ideas by presenting information in a variety of forms *[for example, text, images, tables, sounds]*

3b
to present their completed work effectively *[for example, for public display]*

4a
to review what they have done to help them develop their ideas

4c
to talk about what they might change in future work

5b
exploring a variety of ICT tools *[for example, floor turtle, word processing software, adventure game]*

National Curriculum for England, ICT Programmes of Study

Term 1 Unit of work 1:

Learn selected spellings

Resource Book pages 2–7

Writing Objective

T9: To apply phonological, graphic knowledge and sight vocabulary to spell words accurately.

Links to Sentence/Word Level Work

S3: To recognise and take account of commas and exclamation marks in reading aloud with appropriate expression.

Text Copymasters: C4–C9

Discussing the Text

NB: the story 'Money Doesn't Grow On Trees' is written to incorporate a large number of the words from the Years 1 to 2 list of high frequency words in the NLS Framework document. It is therefore worth noting which words cause problems.

- Introduce the title: 'Money doesn't grow on trees'. Have the children ever come across this expression before? Do they know what it means?
- Read the story on Resource Book pages 2 to 7.
- *Does this story remind you of anything that has happened to you?*
- Discuss how the use of commas and exclamation marks help us to read the story, e.g. commas tell us when to pause, exclamation marks help us to get the right expression in our voices.

Shared Writing

Session 1
Teacher Demonstration

- Children will need their individual whiteboards.
- Tell the children that you have written the first part of a story about another child going shopping for new shoes and that you will want them to spell some of the words for you. (These are underlined in the Shared Writing Example opposite and are words from the Years 1 to 2 list of high frequency words.) Explain to the children that you will ask them to write certain words on their whiteboards.
- Read the whole of the Shared Writing Example out loud and briefly discuss possibilities for how the story might end.
- Write the title of the story.
- *I'm going to start the story by saying 'My mum took me shopping last Saturday'.* Write 'My mum'.

Teacher Scribing

- *The next word I need is 'took'. Write 'took' on your board and then hold it up for me to see.*
- Focus on any mis-spellings and then write 'took', stressing individual phonemes and comparing the word to 'look'.
- *'My mum took'* ... now I need to write 'me shopping last Saturday'. Write 'me shopping'. *See if you can write 'last Saturday' on your board. Sat-ur-day...*
- Focus on any mis-spellings – particularly 'er' for 'ur' in Saturday – and add the words to the sentence.
- *I'm going to finish the sentence by saying 'because I had to have some new shoes for school.'... because is a tricky word – try and write it down.*

Shared Writing Example: Shopping for Shoes

My mum <u>took</u> me shopping <u>last</u> <u>Saturday</u> <u>because</u> I had to <u>have</u> <u>some</u> <u>new</u> shoes for <u>school</u>. I saw my friend who lives in the house <u>next</u> <u>door</u> <u>as</u> we <u>were</u> leaving. I <u>would</u> <u>have</u> liked to stay at <u>home</u> and played <u>with</u> <u>her</u> instead of going shopping <u>with</u> my mum!

<u>When</u> we <u>got</u> to the shop I saw <u>some</u> <u>good</u> shoes. "Those are the <u>ones</u> I <u>want</u>, please Mum! I <u>love</u> <u>them</u>!" Mum <u>laughed</u> and <u>then</u> she said I <u>could</u> not <u>have</u> <u>them because</u> they <u>were</u> pink. "You <u>don't</u> wear pink shoes to <u>school</u>. If you <u>did</u>, you <u>would</u> mess <u>them</u> up on the <u>first</u> day!"

- Ask children to hold up their boards so you can see but don't comment. Write 'because' in the sentence and ask children to compare their version with yours. *Who got it right?* Ask children who wrote the word incorrectly which part they got wrong and what it should have been.
- Complete paragraph one of the Shared Writing Example, with the children using their whiteboards to write the words which are underlined before you add them to the text.
- Read the paragraph through together.

Session 2
Teacher Scribing

- Read the first paragraph through together.
- Write the second paragraph of the Shared Writing Example with the children again using their whiteboards to write the underlined words before you add them to your writing.
- Read the whole piece through together.

Supported Composition

- Ask the children to work in pairs to write two or three sentences to finish off the story.
- Take examples, select and scribe an ending – stress the spellings.

Checking Children's Learning

- Give a class spelling test of the underlined words in the story.

Independent Writing

- Use Copymaster C1 ('Words to Learn') to learn the words which have caused problems

Revisiting the Objective

- Write a different second paragraph for the Shared Writing Example.

Writing Objective

T10: To use story structure to write about own experience in same/similar form.

Links to Sentence/Word Level Work

S5: To revise knowledge about other uses of capitalisation, e.g. for names ... emphasis.

Text Copymasters: C4–C9

Discussing the Text

- Re-read 'Money Doesn't Grow On Trees' (Resource Book pages 2 to 7).
- *Why are some of the words in capital letters?*
- Ask children to share their own experiences of going shopping. Is it something they enjoy? Why/Why not?

Shared Writing

Session 1
Teacher Demonstration

- Have the questions in Shared Writing Example 1 already written out, with spaces in between them for you to write the answers.
- Tell the children that you are going to do some work on planning stories and that you have some questions which will help in planning.
- Read the questions through.
- *First of all we are going to make a plan for 'Money Doesn't Grow on Trees'. That will show us how Wendy Body wrote her story, which will help us when we write ours.*
- Read the first question in Shared Writing Example 1 and then write the answer.

Teacher Scribing

- Complete the remaining questions, using Shared Writing Example 1 to guide children in their answers.
- Read the questions and answers through together and keep the work for the next session.

Session 2
Teacher Scribing

- Have the questions in Shared Writing Example 2 already written out, with spaces in between for you to write the answers.
- Explain to the children that they will be writing a story about going shopping, which you are going to plan together.
- Go through the first five questions, asking for children's suggestions: then select and scribe an answer. Use Shared Writing Example 2 to guide the class.

Supported Composition

- Complete the planning questions, one at a time, with children working in pairs to write answers on their whiteboards. You may like to guide them to a general scenario of the character not being able to find his/her parents.
- Discuss the children's responses, select and scribe.
- Read through the completed plan together.

Shared Writing Example:

1.   2.

Money Doesn't Grow on Trees
Who is the main character in the story? **the child who is telling the story**
Who else is in the story? **the child's mum**
Where does it take place? **at the child's home and in a shopping centre**
How does it begin? **the child doesn't want to go shopping**
What happens next? **the child wants some trainers but Mum says no**
What happens then? **they buy some shoes for school**
What happens next? **the child wants an ice-cream but doesn't think that Mum will buy one**
How does it end? **Mum says they can have ice-creams**

Who is the main character in the story? **a 7 year old child called ...**
Who else is in the story? **the child's mum and dad**
Where does it take place? **at home and then in a big supermarket**
How does it begin? **the child is playing when Dad comes and says that they have to go and do the shopping. The child is cross.**
What happens next? **when they are in the supermarket, the child is bored so slips away and goes to look at the toys**
What happens then?
What happens next?
How does it end?

Then think of a title for the story and write it at the top.

Independent Writing

- Keep the plan on view for children to write the story.
- Use a copy of Copymaster C2, 'Planning a Story', to plan a different story

Checking Children's Learning

- To what extent have the children kept to the plan?
- How much detail have they added?
- *Did having the plan make it easier for you to write your story? Why?*

Revisiting the Objective

- Plan another story to take place in a shopping centre – e.g. where the main character witnesses someone stealing, tells his/her parents and the thief is caught.

Term 1 Unit of work 3:

Structure events in a story

Writing Objective

T11: To use language of time ... to structure a sequence of events.

Links to Sentence/Word Level Work

S2: To find examples of words and phrases that link sentences, e.g. after, meanwhile, during, before, then, next, after a while.

Text Copymasters: C10–C11

Discussing the Text

- Introduce the text 'Jonah's Den' (Resource Book pages 8 to 9), telling the children that they are about to 'read' a story told completely in pictures.
- Go through the comic strip discussing what is happening in each illustration, e.g. *How is the boy feeling in the first picture? What does he do first? What does he do next?*
- *Why did the boy need to untie the washing line?*
- *Why did he need the stones?*
- *Why are his mum and dad cross?*

Shared Writing

Session 1
Teacher Demonstration

- Explain to the children that you are going to write the story told by the pictures.
- *First of all I need to give the boy a name – I can't write a story saying 'the boy' each time. I've decided I'm going to call him Jonah and I'm going to start my story by saying that he is out in the garden and tell my readers how he is feeling.* Write the (Picture 1) text from the Shared Writing Example opposite.
- Ask the children to read back what you have written.
- Look at the second picture and write the next piece of text as a continuation from the first. Commentate, e.g. *I think I shall use some dots here to lead the reader into what Jonah's idea was.*
- Look at the third picture and write the next piece of text. Commentate, e.g. *I'm going to start with 'First of all' because I want to make it easier for the reader to understand the order in which things happened ... I think that if Jonah's mum had seen him taking the sheet she would have stopped him so I'm going to say why this didn't happen ...*

Teacher Scribing

- Look at the fourth illustration. Ask the children what is happening and how you could write it down.
- Discuss suggestions, select and scribe.
- Repeat for pictures 5 and 6.
- Read aloud what you have written so far.
- Ask the children if there is anything they would like to change or improve.

Shared Writing Example

(Picture 1)   Jonah was out in his garden one day. He didn't know what to do and he was feeling very bored.

(Picture 2)   Suddenly, he had a good idea ... he would make a den!

(Picture 3)   First of all, he went indoors to get a sheet. Luckily, his mum was busy so she didn't see him.

(Picture 4)   Jonah had to untie one end of Mum's washing line because it was too high up to make a good tent.

(Picture 5)   After that, he tied the line onto the branch of a tree so that it was lower down. Then he draped the sheet over the line.

(Picture 6)   The only problem was that the sheet just hung down. There was no room inside it like a proper tent.

(Picture 7)   Jonah thought about this, then he went and got a stone from Dad's rockery. He pulled the side of the sheet out and used the stone to keep it in place.

(Picture 8)   It wasn't long before Jonah had collected enough stones to keep both sides of the sheet pulled out. It was just like a real tent.

(Picture 9)   Some time later, Jonah's dad came into the garden. He was really angry when he saw what had happened to his rockery. Then Jonah's mum appeared with a basket of washing she was going to put on the line. She was angry too when she saw what Jonah had done. Meanwhile, Jonah was sitting happily in his tent playing his recorder. He soon stopped though when he heard two cross voices shouting, "JONAH!"

Session 2
Teacher Scribing

- Read what you have written so far.
- Discuss the next part of the story, looking at picture 7. *We could say something like* ... read but don't write the picture 7 text in the Shared Writing Example.

Supported Composition

- Ask children to write down what they think should come next for picture 7.
- Take suggestions, select and scribe.
- Repeat the procedure for picture 8.
- Discuss what could be written for the final picture. Finish the discussion by reading, but not writing, the final example text.

Independent Writing

- Children should write the final part of the story.

Checking Children's Learning

- Share some of the endings.
- Read the complete shared writing. Are there places where sentences could be added to/changed to clarify the sequence of events?

Revisiting the Objective

- Write part of the story in the first person as Jonah.

Writing Objective

T10: To use story structure to write about own experience in same/similar form.

Links to Sentence/Word Level Work

S4: To re-read own writing for sense and punctuation.

Text Copymasters: C10–C11

Discussing the Text

- Remind children how the picture story on Resource Book pages 8 to 9 shows the stages of Jonah making a den and how in the story you wrote together you also made this clear.
- Remind children how words like 'then', 'next', 'first of all', 'after that' can help to make things clear for the reader.

Shared Writing

Session 1
Teacher Demonstration

- Tell the children that they are going to write their own stories about making a den and that today you are going to look at different kinds of den.
- *So, first of all we need to think about the different kinds of den you could make.* Write the title as in Shared Writing Example 1 (opposite). *You could make a tent like Jonah's or a tent using a blanket draped over four chairs or a very simple den with a blanket over a table. I'll write these ideas down so we can think about them.* Write Shared Writing Example 1 – well-spaced to leave room for annotation. Draw attention to how you are using bullet points to set out the list and make it easier to read.

Teacher Scribing

- Ask for any other ideas and add them to the list.
- Discuss each one briefly, especially any potential problems, e.g. having to weight sides to keep them stretched out or the roof taut.
- Annotate the list with reminders as above, or anything special needed to make the den.

Session 2
Teacher Scribing

- Read through the list of ideas from the previous session.
- Explain to the children that today they are going to start writing their own stories about making a den.
- Tell them: *We are going think of some questions that will help you in your writing.*
- Write the title of Shared Writing Example 2 and the first two questions.
- Point out that this time you are numbering the list.
- Ask for further questions – using the Shared Writing Example to guide children if necessary.

1. Ideas for making a den

- a tent like Jonah's
- a tent using a blanket and chairs
- a den under a table with a blanket over the top

2. Writing about the den

1. Who made it?
2. Why?
3. How did you/they make it? What did you/they do first?
4. What did you/they use to make the den?
5. What did you/they do in the den?

Supported Composition

- Read through the list of questions in Shared Writing Example 2.
- Ask the children to jot down their answers to the questions on their whiteboards. Explain that, as this is a story, it doesn't have to be something they have really done. Model answers if necessary, e.g. '1. me, my friend Jake'.
- Children should hold up their boards after each answer for you to see. Help children to correct any mis-spellings you notice.
- Tell the children not to clean off their whiteboards – they will need them for their writing.

Independent Writing

- Children should use their whiteboard notes as reminders to write their stories.

Checking Children's Learning

- Share some of the stories.
- With the Shared Writing Example 2 questions on display, ask the class to check whether or not individuals have covered all these points in their stories.

Revisiting the Objective

- Use the questions to plan a shared story about a tiny little boy, five centimetres high, making a den in someone's house, e.g. using a birthday card in a tent shape, reels of cotton for seats etc.

Term 1 Unit of work 5:

Write rhymes based on the model

Writing Objective

T12: To use simple poetry structures to substitute own ideas.

Text Copymaster Number: C12

Discussing the Text

- Tell children that they are going to read a very simple counting rhyme (which they probably know already).
- Read the first two lines of the rhyme 'Five fat sausages' (Resource Book pages 10 and 11) to model the appropriate rhythm and expression.
- Read the rest of the rhyme together.
- *Look at the illustration – what is happening here?*

Shared Writing

Session 1
Teacher Demonstration

- Explain that you are going to write a similar counting rhyme together but it is going to be about balloons. Write the title – see the Shared Writing Example opposite.
- *When a balloon bursts, it could go BANG! But I don't want to use the same word as in the sausages rhyme, so I'm going to have the balloons going POP! That means that I've got to have a word which rhymes with POP at the end of the first line.* Pause for thinking ... *shop would be a good word to use ...* Pause for thinking ... *I've decided, this is what I'm going to write.* Write the first line of the example and read it aloud.
- Write the second line of the example but without the crossing out. *Do you know, I think I could make this line more interesting ... I could change 'All of a sudden' to 'suddenly' and say what colour the balloon was.* Cross out the line and write the new version as in the Shared Writing Example.
- Write the next couplet as in the Shared Writing Example. As you get to 'green', explain that you need a one-syllable colour, otherwise it won't fit the line.

Teacher Scribing

- Together, read aloud the lines written so far.
- Ask the children what you should write for the remaining lines and scribe.
- Work together to compose a final line as in the example.
- Read the whole rhyme.

Session 2
Teacher Scribing

- Tell the children that you want them to compose another counting rhyme. *It's going to be about open doors that are waiting to be slammed and the wind comes along and slams the first one shut with a bang and then the second one and so on.*
- Ask for suggestions for the first line, e.g. 'Five open doors waiting to be slammed,' and scribe.
- Ask for suggestions for the second line, e.g. 'Along came the wind and the first went BANG!' and scribe.

Five big balloons

Five big balloons carried out from the shop,

~~All of a sudden, one went POP!~~

Suddenly the red one just went POP!

Four big balloons carried out from the shop,

Suddenly the green one just went POP!

Three big balloons carried out from the shop,

Suddenly the blue one just went POP!

Two big balloons carried out from the shop,

Suddenly the white one just went POP!

One big balloon carried out from the shop,

Suddenly that last one just went POP!

So now there were no balloons left in the shop!

Supported Composition

- Ask children to use their whiteboards to compose the next two lines about the *second* door.
- Continue with the rest of the rhyme.

Independent Writing

- Children write and illustrate the balloons or doors rhyme – without the shared versions on view. Some children may like to make up their own rhymes. (See the suggestion below in 'Revisiting the objective'.)

Checking Children's Learning

- Have children maintained structure and rhyme in their versions?
- Were they able to spell the words they needed?

Revisiting the Objective

- Substitute 'fat sausages frying' for 'boiled eggs bubbling'.

Writing Objective

T12: Use simple poetry structures and ... write new lines

Text Copymasters: C14–C15

Discussing the Text

- Tell the children that they are going to read another very simple counting rhyme. This one is called 'Fishes in the sea!'.
- Read to the class the rhyme on Resource Book pages 12 and 13.
- *How important are the illustrations? Would the rhyme make sense without the pictures?*
- *How is this counting rhyme different from the 'Five Fat Sausages' rhyme that we read before?* (Recap by reading the rhyme on Resource Book page 10.)

Shared Writing

- **NB: Rather than carry this unit's work over two sessions, it is suggested that you have one extended 30-minute session.**

Teacher Demonstration

- Tell the children that you are going to continue the rhyme together, but first of all you need to think about the pattern or structure of the rhyme.
- Write Shared Writing Example 1 (opposite) and discuss it with the class.
- Explain that you have decided to write the next part about the three fishes talking about going home at the end of the show and that you are going to start with ten and go backwards. *The difficult part will be thinking of rhymes to go with the numbers.*
- Write: Ten, nine, eight. *Which word have I got to find a rhyme for? Yes, eight ... I've thought of one so I'm going to write 'It's getting very ...' What word shall I put in here? Yes, 'late'.*

Teacher Scribing

- *How do I start the next line? Yes, 'Seven, six, five'. Who can spell 'seven' for me?* Write 'Seven, six, five'. *Which word have I got to find a rhyme for? Yes, five ... I'm going to write 'It's time for us to'.* Write it. *Who can tell me what word could go here? Yes 'dive' makes sense and rhymes with 'five' so I'll put that.*
- Do the next line in a similar way (See Shared Writing Example 2).
- Tell the children that you are going to start the last two lines and then they will finish them off. Remind them that there should be 10 syllables in the first of these lines and 13 in the second. The lines must rhyme. Write:

  And off swam two fish leaving [space]
  who went and told [space]

Supported Composition

- Children should complete the two lines, working in pairs on their whiteboards.
- Share children's efforts and then select and scribe to complete the poem.

Shared Writing Example

1.

- goes from 1 to 10
- three numbers at a time
- which words have to rhyme?
- how many syllables in the last two lines?

2.

Ten, nine, eight, 'It's getting very (late).'

Seven, six, five. 'It's time for us to (dive)!'

Four, three, two, 'We'll say goodbye to (you)!'

And off swam two fish leaving (only one)

who went and told (his mum and dad all about the fun.)

Independent Writing

- Children should work in pairs or groups to compose their own counting rhymes. They can choose one of the following forms:
  - One, two, three ....
  - Ten, nine, eight, ...
  - One, two .... (as in 'buckle my shoe')
  - One ....
    Along came another one and that made two.

Checking Children's Learning

- Have children maintained structure and rhyme in their chosen form?
- Were they able to spell the words they needed?
- What did they find easy/difficult about writing the rhyme?

Revisiting the Objective

- Write a rhyme together using the following as a starting point:
    One tiny monster, sitting in a shoe
    Along came another one and that made two.

Term 1 Unit of work 7:

Find the missing words and spell them

Resource Book
pages 14–19

Writing Objective

T12: To apply phonological, graphic knowledge and sight vocabulary to spell words accurately.

Text Copymasters: C16–C24

Discussing the Text

- Explain to the children that they are about to read an extract from 'Little Red Riding Hood' but *some of the words are missing so we'll have to guess what they are as we read.*
- Read through the extract on Resource Book pages 14 to 19 asking the children to supply the words that are missing from each verse (See Shared Writing Example 1, opposite).

Shared Writing

Session 1
Teacher Demonstration

- Clip the acetate sheet to page 14.
- Explain that you want to see if the children can spell the missing words, but that you are going to start them off.
- Write in the missing words in the first verse. (See Shared Writing Example).

Teacher Scribing

- Clean off the acetate. Decide what the first missing word might be in verse 2 and ask the children to tell you how to spell it. Then write it in.
- Complete the verse. What do the children notice about two of the words you have written? (vowel modified by 'e'/finale/'magic e' words.)
- Clean off the acetate. Scribe the missing words in the third verse.
- Clean off/remove the acetate.
- Return to any of the words which caused problems, and ask the children to spell them again.

Session 2
Supported Composition

- Remind the children what you were doing in the previous session.
- Explain that this time the children are to write down the words on their whiteboards instead of you doing it.
- Have a piece of paper handy so that you can jot down any of the words that cause problems.
- Decide what the first missing word might be in verse 4. Ask the children to write it and hold up their boards for you to see.
- Complete the verse and the remainder of the extract.
- Choose other words from the text, e.g. happily, somebody, wearing, naughty, opened, straight, and see if children can spell/write them.

Checking Children's Learning

- Give a class spelling test of the more difficult words you have been focusing on.

The missing words

Verse 1	**Verse 2**	**Verse 3**
little	made	girl
was	smell	put
was	Take	off
old	well	house
		away

Verse 4	**Verse 5**	**Verse 6**
walked	hungry	through
by	girl	house
with	hood	shouted
look	licked	when
	could	door
		bin

Independent Writing

- Use Copymaster C1, 'Words to Learn', to learn the words which have caused problems.

Revisiting the Objective

- Use the next extract from Little Red Riding Hood on pages 20 to 22. Mask the words you want to focus on with 'sausages' of Blu-tack.

Term 1 Unit of work 8:

Write a character profile

Resource Book pages 20–23

Writing Objective

T14: To write character profiles eg simple descriptions using key words and phrases that describe or are spoken by characters in the text.

Links to Sentence/Word Level Work

S9: To secure the use of simple sentences in own writing.

Text Copymaster: C25

Discussing the Text

- Introduce the extract, telling the children that it is another piece from 'Little Red Riding Hood'.
- Read together the text on Resource Book pages 20 to 22.
- *Why is the wolf trying to get Red Riding Hood to come closer?*
- *How do we know that the wolf is getting cross and impatient?*

Shared Writing

Session 1
Teacher Scribing

- Have the acetate sheet clipped to page 23, 'A Character Portrait of the Wolf'.
- Tell the children that you are going to be writing a character description of the wolf based on what it says in the text and what is shown in the illustrations. First of all you are going to make notes on this.
- Go through the text identifying relevant phrases etc., and scribe on the frame as in Shared Writing Example 1, opposite. Guide the children to the last two bullet points.
- *Look at the illustrations – do they tell us anything else about the wolf?* Scribe as in the second part of Shared Writing Example 1.
- Read what has been written.

Teacher Demonstration

- Explain that you are now going to write a description of the wolf using your notes. *I want you to watch carefully while I write it and see if you can work out what I am doing.*
- Write Shared Writing Example 2, then read it aloud.
- See if the children can tell you that you have rearranged the notes to put all the information about the wolf's appearance first and the information about his personality second. If they haven't realised this, you should point it out.
- Tell the children that in the next session you will be looking at this description to see if you can improve it.

Session 2
Teacher Demonstration

- Re-read the description.
- *Let's look at this first sentence: 'The wolf had grey fur with a white chest and his paws were white and hairy too.'... I think it would be better if I cut some of this out and just said 'The wolf had grey fur with a white chest and white, hairy paws.'* Cross out and insert text as in Example 3.

A Character Portrait of the Wolf

1. What we can tell from the text:
- hairy paws
- beady eyes
- pointed teeth
- could pretend to be nice
- could get cross and impatient

What we can tell from the illustrations:
- pointed ears
- grey fur
- white chest and paws

2. The wolf had grey fur with a white chest and his paws were white and hairy too. He had little beady eyes below his pointed ears and sharp pointed teeth. The wolf could pretend to be nice but he could also get cross and impatient.

3. The wolf had grey fur with a white chest and white, hairy paws. ~~his paws were white and hairy too.~~ Below his pointed ears ~~H~~he had little beady eyes ~~below his pointed ears~~ and sharp pointed teeth. When he wanted something, ~~T~~the wolf could pretend to be nice, but he could also get cross and impatient when he didn't get his own way.

- *Let's look at the next sentence: 'He had little beady eyes below his pointed ears and sharp pointed teeth.' ... I think it would sound better if I started the sentence with 'below his pointed ears' ... 'Below his pointed ears he had little beady eyes and sharp pointed teeth.' Do you think that sounds better? I do.* Cross out and insert text as in Example 3.
- *Let's read the last sentence: 'The wolf could pretend to be nice but he could also get cross and impatient.' I haven't said when or why the wolf was nice ... When did he pretend to be nice? ... Yes, when he wanted something. And when did he get cross and impatient? That's right – when he wasn't getting his own way. Now add those things to my sentence.*

Supported Composition
- The children write a new version of the final sentence.
- Compare versions, select and amend your own final sentence. Read the complete description.

Independent Writing
- Children should use the illustrations and their own guesses to write a character description of Little Red Riding Hood.

Checking Children's Learning
- Share descriptions: can children suggest ways of improving them?

Revisiting the Objective
- Use one child's description to work on together.

Describe the setting for a story

Writing Objective

T13: To use story settings from reading, e.g. re-describe, use in own writing.

Links to Sentence/Word Level Work

S3: To re-read own writing to check for grammatical sense (coherence) and accuracy (agreement).

Text Copymasters: C26–C29

Discussing the Text

- Tell the children that they are going to hear an extract from a story that describes a magical cave.
- Read to the children the extract on Resource Book pages 24 to 27. Explain any unfamiliar vocabulary, e.g. 'gasped', 'granite' (page 24).
- *What does the writer say about the cave which makes you want to see it for yourself?*
- Discuss how the writer makes a contrast between the cave as it *was* (e.g. clumps of seaweed, dark and gloomy, page 24), and the cave as it is *now* (e.g. beautiful flowers, soft light, page 26).

Shared Writing

Session 1
Teacher Scribing

- Explain that the children are going to write their own description of the cave.
- *First of all I want you to help me make a list of the things which the writer mentions about the cave that we must include in our description. Let's start with the cave as it was when Estelle had seen it before.*
- Write 'Before'. Ask children to identify the appropriate parts of the text and scribe as in Shared Writing Example 1 (opposite).
- Write 'Now'. Ask children to identify the appropriate parts of the text and scribe as in the Shared Writing Example.
- Read the list through. (**NB:** Keep the list for Session 2.)

Teacher Demonstration

- *I'm going to start the description of the cave and then you will finish it off tomorrow/in our next writing session. I'm going to describe the cave as it was when Estelle had seen it before.*
- Scribe Shared Writing Example 2. Comment on the following in particular:
  - the use of commas
  - the linking of seaweed and pools, making it dangerous to walk
  - the use of 'But' at the beginning of a sentence for emphasis.
- Read the description with the children.

Session 2
Teacher Scribing

- Remind children of Session 1 and display the list of descriptive features.
- Read the first part of the description (see Shared Writing Example 2).
- Write Shared Writing Example 3. Tell the children that they are going to help write the rest of the description using the list to help them, but that they should try and add some details of their own.

1. Before:
   - dark, damp and gloomy place
   - dark granite walls
   - hidden pools
   - clumps of slippery seaweed

Now:
   - soft glow of light coming from inside.
   - walls were sparkling
   - soft glowing light
   - smooth golden sand
   - silver path
   - strange but beautiful flowers
   - large heavy door
   - *What other details can you add?*

2. When Estelle had seen the cave before, it had been a dark, damp and gloomy place with granite walls. Clumps of slippery seaweed and hidden pools had made it difficult to walk safely. But now the cave was completely different.

3. The first thing she saw was soft glow of light coming from inside. Then she noticed that

Supported Composition
   - Children should work in pairs to compose the first sentence orally.
   - Take some examples and discuss them briefly.
   - Repeat with the next sentence.

Independent Writing
   - Children should write a complete description of the magical cave.

Checking Children's Learning
   - Have children included all the features on the list? Have they added details of their own?

Revisiting the Objective
   - Write a shared description of a magical underwater cave.

Term 1 Unit of work 10:

Write a story

Writing Objective

T13: To use story settings from reading, e.g. write a different story in the same setting.

Links to Sentence/Word Level Work

S5: To use verb tenses with increasing accuracy, e.g. see/saw, go/went and to use past tense consistently for narration.

Text Copymasters: C26–C29

Discussing the Text

- Remind the children about the extract, 'A Magical Cave' (Resource Book pages 24 to 27) and how it was about a cave that had been transformed by some kind of magic. Stress that an ordinary setting had been changed into a very special one.

Shared Writing

Session 1
Teacher Demonstration

- Tell the children that they are going to plan and write a story of their own about a magical cave.
- *Here are some questions which will help us plan a story.* Write Shared Writing Example 1.
- Go through the questions and discuss possibilities, e.g. *Where was the cave? On a hillside? Near the sea? Underground?*
- Tell the children that you are going to write the start of a story about a cave.
- Write Shared Writing Example 2.

Teacher Scribing

- Ask for suggestions as to how the story might develop and list them in broad terms, e.g. 'A dwarf takes you to his cave to help his dog, which has a thorn in its paw'. Take time out for the children to discuss this briefly in pairs first of all.
- Tell the children that they will be writing their own stories in the next writing session.

Session 2
Teacher Scribing

- Go through the planning questions and suggested story outlines. Explain that the children can make their own choice and that they do not need to use any of the suggestions if they can think of a better one – but it must be about a *magical* cave.
- Give the class approximately a minute's silent thinking time during which children should think about how they could start their story and what will happen. They can use your idea for an opening if they wish.

Shared Writing Example

1 Who discovered the cave? How?
Where was it?
What did it look like? What was magical about it?
What happened in the cave?

2 It was a lovely summer's day and I had been out walking on the hills. I was tired so I sat down to rest. I was so tired that I must have fallen asleep. The next thing I knew was that someone was shaking my arm. A voice said, "Wake up! Come with me. You've got to help me!"
I looked round and saw

Supported Composition
- Individually, children should write the opening sentences for their story. This should be done in notebooks, with children seated at their tables.
- Discuss one or two of the openings and ask your more reluctant writers if they know how they are going to continue.

Independent Writing
- Children write their stories.
- They should share their work within their groups and help each other to check if they have used verb tenses properly, e.g. see/saw, go/went .

Checking Children's Learning
- Have the children written about a *magical* cave as directed, or an ordinary one?
- Have children used the past tense consistently for their stories?

Revisiting the Objective
- Plan a story together using one of the suggested storylines from Session 1.

Term 1 Unit of work 11:

Add verses to a poem

Writing Objective

T15: To use structures from poems as a basis for writing by extending or substituting elements, inventing own lines, verses.

Text Copymasters: C30–33

Discussing the Text

- Introduce the poem 'The Inside–Outside Man' (Resource Book pages 28 to 31) and tell the children that they are going to read a nonsense poem.
- Read the poem aloud together and discuss the children's reactions.
- *How do you think the man feels about his van?*
- *What makes this a nonsense poem?*
- Identify the rhyming pattern, i.e. second and fourth lines rhyme.

Shared Writing

Session 1
Teacher Demonstration

- Tell the children that you are going to invent some more verses for the poem. *Let's imagine that the Inside–Outside man is lonely living by himself and that he'd like to find a girlfriend and get married ...*
- Write the first 2 lines of the Shared Writing Example. Read them aloud.
- *I think he would want someone who loved his van as much as he does so for the next line I'm going to write 'and if she makes friends with Matilda,' ...*

Teacher Scribing

- Read the first three lines, stressing 'life'. *What could I put for the last line? It needs to fit the rhythm of the poem (de-dum-de-de-dum-de-dum-dum) and rhyme with what?*
- Take suggestions and scribe along the lines of the Shared Writing Example.
- *Now let's have a verse about what she looks like. We could start it like this: 'She would have to have beautiful eyes,' ... Bearing in mind that the Inside–Outside man likes things that are mixed up, do you think he'd like her to have two eyes the same colour or eyes which are two different colours – say one brown one and one green one? What could we write next?* Take suggestions and scribe along the lines of the Shared Writing Example.
- Continue prompting and guiding children using the Shared Writing Example to complete the second verse.
- Read the two verses and tell the children that you will write some more in the next session.

Session 2
Teacher Scribing

- Read the two verses you have written so far.
- Prompt and guide the children, using the Shared Writing Example, to write the third verse.

Shared Writing Example

I'm hoping to meet a young lady,
who will share my back-to-front life,
and if she makes friends with Matilda,
I'll ask her if she'll be my wife.

She would have to have beautiful eyes,
one brown one and one that is green,
with straight and curly mixed-up hair
and the kindest smile I have seen.

She'll like all the same things that I do,
she'll live in a back-to-front house.
She might have a topsy-turvy dog
or a cat with its own pet mouse.

Yes, I'm hoping to meet a young lady,
who'll say that she'll be my wife,
and we'll be happy together,
sharing our back-to-front life.

Supported Composition
• Help the children to write a concluding verse, one line at a time using the example for guidance.

Independent Writing
• Ask children to work in pairs to write another verse about the way the young lady dresses.
• Share and display some of the children's work.

Checking Children's Learning
• Have children kept to the spirit of the poem?
• Have they maintained the rhythm and rhyming pattern?

Revisiting the Objective
• Write a verse or two about the couple's wedding day.

NB Keep the work from this unit – it will be needed in Unit 12.

Term 1 Unit of work 12:

Write character descriptions

Writing Objective

T14: To write character profiles eg simple descriptions using key words and phrases that describe or are spoken by characters in the text.

Links to Sentence/Word Level Work

S3: To re-read own writing to check for grammatical sense (coherence) and accuracy (agreement).

Text Copymasters: C30–C33

Discussing the Text

- Tell the children that they are going to write a character description of the Inside–Outside man and that you need to read the poem again in order to remind yourselves about him.
- Read the poem aloud (Resource Book pages 28 to 31), pausing to comment on verses which describe the way he looks, his van and his house.

Shared Writing

Session 1
Teacher Demonstration

- Explain that the character description should cover what the man looks like, what he is like as a person and the things that are important to him.
- Tell the children that you are going to start with the way the man looks. Write Shared Example 1, commenting as you write, e.g. *I'm starting with an introductory sentence, which says that the man dressed in a strange way and then I'll go on to explain what I mean by that … The poem says his socks go on over his boots but I'll change that to say he put his boots on before his socks because I think it sounds better in a character description …*
- Read the description through together.

Teacher Scribing

- *Now we need to say something about what kind of man he is. The poem doesn't actually tell us this, but I think that people probably laughed at him because he looked so funny – but I don't think he would mind because he seems a very happy and cheerful sort of person, doesn't he?*
- Ask for suggestions as to what you should write next.
- Discuss, select and scribe.
- Discuss, select and scribe anything else the children want to add.
- Read the description through together. Ask the children if there is anything that they would like to change and check for punctuation.

Session 2
Teacher Scribing

- Read the description through together. Ask the children if they are still happy with it or if there are changes they would like to make.
- Explain that you need a sentence to link the first part of the description with the next and write Shared Writing Example 3.

1. The Inside–Outside man dressed in a very strange way. He wore ordinary clothes, but he put them on the wrong way round. His shirts were back to front, his suits were inside-out and he always put his boots on before his socks.

2. People laughed when they saw him but the Inside–Outside man didn't mind because he was a very cheerful and happy man.

3 There were two things that the Inside–Outside man loved. One was his van and the other was his house.

Supported Composition
- Ask the children to write a sentence about the Inside–Outside man's van and how he felt about it. *If you wanted to, you could start your sentence with 'The Inside–Outside man loved his van because ...'*
- Look at the children's sentences, select and scribe – amending if needs be to incorporate more than one suggestion.
- Ask the children to write one or two sentences about the Inside–Outside man's house. *Why did he like it? Was it because it was all mixed up like him?*
- Again, discuss the children's sentences, select and scribe – amending if needs be to incorporate more than one suggestion.
- Read the entire description. Ask the children if there is anything that they would like to change or that they think needs changing.

Independent Writing
- The children should use the poem about the young lady the Inside–Outside man would like to meet to write a character description of her. They may invent further details if they wish.

Checking Children's Learning
- Have the children organised their descriptions in a similar way to the Shared Writing description?
- Does the writing show evidence of reading and checking for sense and accuracy? Are there corrections or omissions, for example?

Revisiting the Objective
- Add another few sentences to the description, inventing details about the Inside–Outside man's likes and dislikes, e.g. food or hobbies.

Writing Composition Objective

T15: To write own poems from initial jottings and words.

Text Copymasters: C30–C33

Shared Writing

Session 1
Teacher Demonstration

- Remind the children of 'The Inside–Outside Man' by reading again the poem on pages 28 to 31.
- *Let's imagine that the Inside–Outside man married his girlfriend and that they eventually had a baby – a little boy who is now eight years old.* Tell the children that you are going to write a poem about their son at school.
- *I'm going to start our poem with a verse which is very like the one about the boy's dad ...* Write the first verse of the Shared Writing Example. Read it aloud.
- *Now we need to say something about the boy's school, so for the next verse I'm going to write this ...* Write the first three lines of the second verse of the Shared Writing Example.

Teacher Scribing

- Read the three lines, stressing 'tree'. *What could I put for the last line? It needs to fit the rhythm of the poem and rhyme with what? Yes 'tree'.*
- Take suggestions, prompting if necessary, and scribe along the lines of the Shared Writing Example.
- *Now let's have a verse about something the boy likes doing at school. We could start it like this: 'On Wednesdays we always play football'... Do you think they would use a round ball or a square one in this mixed-up school?*
- Take suggestions and scribe the first two lines along the lines of the Shared Writing Example.
- Continue prompting and guiding children (using the Shared Writing Example if they get stuck) to complete the third verse.
- Read the three verses and tell the children that you will write some more in the next session.

Session 2
Teacher Scribing

- Read the verses you have written so far.
- *I think we should continue the poem by saying something about what the boy wears when he plays football. If his dad wears his trousers up to his knees, how do you think this mixed-up boy might wear his football shorts?*
- Prompt and guide the children, using the example to write the fourth verse.

Supported Composition

- Help the children to write a concluding verse, one line at a time using the

The Inside–Outside Boy

I'm back to front and I'm all mixed up,
I'm just like my mum and my dad.
I'm an inside–outside, under and over,
backwards and forwards lad.

I go to a brilliant mixed-up school
where my teacher sits in a tree,
and the playground up on the roof
is a sight you really should see.

On Wednesdays we always play football
with a ball that's square and not round.
And if there's a chance of us winning,
I stop for a snooze on the ground.

I wear my shorts down to my ankles,
my sock goes on over my boot,
my shirt is always on back to front –
I face the wrong way when I shoot.

Yes I'm back to front and all mixed up,
I'm the inside–outside lad,
like my inside–outside, under and over,
backwards and forwards dad.

example for guidance.

Independent Writing

- Children work in pairs or groups to write another verse or two about the Inside–Outside boy at school. Get children started by asking questions, e.g. *What lessons does he like? What does he do at playtime? What is his best friend like?* Ask them to jot down ideas and useful words/phrases before they start.

Checking Children's Learning

- *How useful did you find the ideas and words that you jotted down before you started to make up your verse?*
- Have children kept to the spirit of the poem?
- Have they maintained the rhythm and rhyming pattern?

Term 1 Unit of work 14:

Write a story with correct spellings

Resource Book pages 32–37

Writing Objective

T9: To apply phonological, graphic knowledge and sight vocabulary to spell words accurately.

Links to Sentence/Word Level Work

S2: The need for grammatical agreement, matching verbs to nouns/pronouns.

Text Copymasters: C34–C39

Discussing the Text

- Introduce and read the story 'Strange Bumps' (Resource Book pages 32 to 37).
- *How soon did you guess what the two strange bumps were?*
- *What was Owl afraid might happen?*
- *How would you describe Owl?*

Shared Writing

Session 1
Teacher Demonstration

- Explain to the children that they are going to write a story based on Arnold Lobel's story about an owl, but that it will be about a mouse. Keep the Lobel text on view as support in structuring the story.
- The emphasis in this unit is on spelling, so ask the children to help you with spelling words during demonstration and scribing – for example, the words which are underlined in the Shared Writing Example. You may also like to make a few deliberate spelling mistakes.
- *I'm going to start the story off for you. The title I've thought of is 'A Strange Thing in the Bed' so I'll just write that down. I'm going to begin the story with Mouse deciding it was time to go to bed …*
- Write the Shared Writing Example modelling re-reading as you write.
- Ask the children to read the beginning of the story with you.
- *Can you guess what the strange thing in the bed will be? Yes, Mouse's tail!*

Teacher Scribing

- *What will happen now? Is this where Mouse first spots the strange thing in the bed? What shall I write next?*
- Take suggestions, discuss and scribe a sentence about Mouse noticing something in the bed.
- *Now what? Do you think he might ask himself what that strange thing could be? What will he imagine that it might be? … (a snake?)*
- Take suggestions, discuss and scribe.
- Continue with the story as time permits but leave time to read the writing and see if there is anything that needs checking or changing.

Session 2
Teacher Scribing

- Read the story so far.
- Continue with the next sentence of the story taking suggestions, discussing and scribing. Take time out for children to discuss possibilities briefly in pairs beforehand.

A Strange Thing in the Bed

<u>Mouse</u> was very sleepy so he decided that it was <u>time</u> to go to bed. He went <u>upstairs</u> and brushed his <u>teeth</u>. Then he pulled back the <u>blanket</u> and climbed into bed. He was just going to <u>blow</u> out the candle when he noticed that there was <u>something</u> in the bed.

"What is that thing in the bed with me?" <u>asked</u> Mouse.

Mouse peeped under the blanket but it was too dark to see <u>anything</u>. He <u>tried</u> to go to sleep but he <u>couldn't</u>. Mouse twitched his <u>tail</u>.

Supported Composition

- Children should write the next two or three sentences, one at a time, on their whiteboards. Make a selection for scribing.
- Read the story so far and discuss what remains to be done. Remind them how Lobel finishes the story.

Independent Writing

- The children should finish off the story.
- Direct them to go through their work when they have finished and check not only for sense but also to check the spelling – they should read twice in order to concentrate on one aspect at a time.

Checking Children's Learning

- How successful are the endings?
- Have children kept to the original Lobel structure/concept? For example, 'Let it wiggle as much as it likes …'
- Have children been able to identify any spelling errors? (Don't expect them to identify all of them!)

Revisiting the Objective

- Present children with a version of the Shared Writing Example with lots of spelling mistakes for them to spot and correct.

Term 1 Unit of work 15:

Write tongue twisters

Writing Objective

T11: To write tongue twisters or alliterative sentences.

Links to Sentence/Word Level Work

S4: To use commas in lists.

Text Copymasters: C40–C41

Discussing the Text

- Tell the children that today you are going to look at two pictures which will help you write some tongue twisters. Explain, if the children don't already know, that *a tongue twister is a rhyme or sentence where most of the words begin with the same sound.*
- Look at the illustration on the page headed 'Writing Tongue Twisters!' (Resource Book page 38) and ask the children to describe what is going on.
- *Which two sounds do you think the picture is about?* (s and t).
- Look at the illustration on page 39 and ask children to describe what is happening in that one.
- *Which two sounds do you think this picture is about?* (r and f).

Shared Writing

Session 1
Teacher Scribing

- *Look carefully at this picture on page 38 again and tell me all the things which begin with a 't' sound. I'll write them down as you say them.* List things as children identify them. (A horizontal list allows a teaching opportunity on using commas in lists.) Read the list.
- Repeat with the things beginning with 's'.

Teacher Demonstration

- *I'm going to take some of the words from the lists which I think could make a good tongue twister and write them here ...* Write Shared Writing Example 1. *Look, there are two words here which rhyme. What are they? Yes, 'tea' and 'sea'. I'm going to make up a rhyming tongue twister with these words and I might add a couple more which aren't there – see if you can spot them.*
- Write Shared Writing Example 2. Read it to the children and then ask them to read it back to you.

Supported Composition

- Ask the children to make up a sentence using words from the 's' or the 't' list. They can add other words beginning with their chosen letter if they wish.
- Share some of the sentences. Focus, in particular, on those sentences that do not use too many words beginning with other letters.

Session 2
Teacher Scribing

- *Look carefully at this picture on page 39 and tell me all the things which begin with an 'r' sound. I'll write them down as you say them.* List things as children identify them. Read the list.

- Repeat with the things beginning with 'f'.
- Pull out and list some useful phrases – see Shared Writing Example 3.

Shared Writing Example

1. two tigers, tortoise, tea
sea, six seals, sailing

2. Two tired tigers and a tortoise take tea
as six silly seals sail slowly on the sea.

3. red robots
running races
rushing round
five fairies falling
fat fairy
flying fast

Supported Composition
- Ask the children to use the lists to make up and write a tongue twister sentence for the letter 'r'.
- Take suggestions. Write up a couple of the examples which use too many words beginning with other letters and see if you can work together to make them more alliterative.
- Ask children to use the lists to make up and write a tongue twister sentence for the letter 'f'.
- Take suggestions and, again, work on a couple together to improve the alliteration.

Independent Writing
- Tell the children that you are going to make a class book/class posters of tongue twisters. Children should work in pairs to draft three tongue twisters using three different letters. More able children might try a rhyming tongue twister using two letters as in Session 1. Final versions should be written on strips of coloured paper for later pasting up.

Checking Children's Learning
- Have children understood the concept of a tongue twister, i.e. have they avoided using too many words beginning with other letters?

Revisiting the Objective
- Write tongue twisters about food, e.g. 'Charlie chews chicken and chips.'

Writing Objective

T10: To write sustained stories using knowledge of story elements: narrative, settings, characterisation, dialogue and the language of story.

Text Copymasters: C42–C43

Discussing the Text

- Explain that Resource Book pages 40 and 41 are designed to help them plan a story.
- Go through the headings to establish that the children understand them.

Shared Writing

Session 1
Teacher Demonstration

NB: It is advisable not to use the acetate over the text for this session, since you will need to keep the story plan on view for the whole of the time that the children are writing their stories.

- Tell the children that you are going to plan a story together and that it is going to be a retelling of a fairy tale that they might know already. *A 'retelling' means that we can make changes to the story if we want to.*
- *I'm going to start off our plan by saying who the main characters will be. It says* **character** *here* [singular], *but our story has* **two** *characters who are both important.*
- Write Shared Writing Example 1 (opposite), but leave out the names. *So our two characters are a boy and a girl who are brother and sister. Can you guess which fairy tale we are planning?* Depending on the children's response, either confirm by writing in the names or give a clue by writing in one name to begin with.
- Ask the children what they remember about the story of Hansel and Gretel.

Teacher Scribing

- Ask the children which other characters appear in the story and scribe.
- Ask what you should say about the setting. Ensure that you guide the class to saying that the story begins in the children's cottage, moves to the wood and then to the Gingerbread House belonging to the witch.
- *'How will the story start?'* – make sure that the children understand that this requires notes (bullet points?) on the first part of the story and not the actual opening. It will probably go as far as the point where Hansel and Gretel first see the Gingerbread House.
- Plan the rest of the story in note form. You could highlight opportunities for dialogue and include one piece as a model.

Session 2
Teacher Scribing

- Read through the plan and tell the children that you are going to help them with the opening to their stories.
- *I'm going to read you one way of opening the story. Listen carefully and then we'll decide if that is the sort of thing we want to write.*
- Read Shared Writing Example 2 (below).
- *What did you think of that? Was it a good way to start the story?*
- Ask children what you should write for your opening. Take suggestions and scribe.

Shared Writing Example

1. An eight year old boy called Hansel
His six year old sister called Gretel

2. Once upon a time there were two children who lived with their father in a cottage at the edge of the wood. Their names were Hansel and Gretel. The two children were very happy until the day that their father got married again. Their new stepmother did not like children and she was very cruel to Hansel and Gretel.

Independent Writing
NB: This should be spread over more than one session

- The children should now follow the plan and write the story up to the point where Hansel and Gretel first see the Gingerbread House.
- Stop and review what the children have written and then recap on what they should be writing next – the 'What will happen in the middle?' section.
- The children write this part of the story.
- Review what the children have written and then recap on what they should be writing in the final section.
- The children should read their work and see if changes need to be made.

Checking Children's Learning

- How successfully have the children followed the plan?
- Did they find it helped them?
- Were they able to maintain consistency of person and tense?

Revisiting the Objective

- Plan another well-known story for children to re-tell.

Writing Objective

T11: To use humorous verse as a structure to write own by adaptation, mimicry or substitution.

Links to Sentence/Word Level Work

S2: The need for grammatical agreement, matching verbs to nouns/pronouns.

Text Copymasters: C44–C45

Discussing the Text

- Tell the children that they are going to hear two funny poems.
- Read both limericks on Resource Book pages 42 and 43.
- *This kind of nonsense poem is called a limerick. Look at the two we have here. How does a limerick usually start? How many lines does a limerick have? How many syllables are there in each line?*
- Explain to the children that they are going to help you write limericks and then have a go at writing limericks for themselves.

Shared Writing

Session 1
Teacher Demonstration

- *If we are going to write our own limericks, we need to remind ourselves exactly what a limerick is.* Write Shared Writing Example 1 (opposite). Go through it briefly and then keep it on view.
- *The first limerick we are going to write starts like this, 'There was a young lady called Rose '... Have I got the right number of syllables in the first line? ... Now I'm going to write, 'Who painted her knees and her ...' What word could I put in here which rhymes with 'Rose'?*
- Continue writing the rest of the limerick in Shared Writing Example 2, asking children to supply the final word at the end of lines 4 and 5 and getting them to check the number of syllables. You could write 'her whole head' and then cross out 'whole' when children discover there are six instead of five syllables.
- Read the limerick together.

Session 2
Teacher Demonstration and Scribing

- Remind children of the structure of limericks using the Shared Writing Example 1 sheet from the previous session.
- Write Shared Writing Example 3 as you did Example 2. Get children to supply the parts that are underlined – giving clues and prompting as necessary, e.g. *Where do you usually find baby birds before they can fly?*

Supported Composition

- Write Shared Writing Example 4. Tell the children that this time they are going to make up the limerick for themselves, but that you will give them some rhyming words to help them.
- Write Shared Writing Example 5.
- Children should work in pairs to write the second line. Sample their efforts, check line length and rhyme and ask what they think they will write next.

1. Limericks
- nonsense poems
- usually start with 'There was a ...'
- five lines
- lines 1, 2 and 5 rhyme with each other
- lines 3 and 4 rhyme with each other
- number of syllables in a line: 8, 8, 5, 5, 8

2.
There was a young lady called Rose
Who painted her knees and her toes.
   She painted her head
   A very bright red
With blue and white stripes on her nose!

3.
There was a young bird in <u>a nest,</u>
Who said, "I am really <u>the best!</u>
   One day <u>very soon,</u>
   I'll fly <u>to the moon</u> –
I won't even stop <u>for a rest!</u>"

4. There was a young bird in a tree

5. see, bee, me, hee hee, pea, sea, tea, flea

Independent Writing
- Children complete their limerick on their whiteboards and check that they have got the form and rhymes right. They should then write a fair copy on paper for display.
- Children compose their own limericks, working in pairs and drafting on their whiteboards. Writing limericks is not simple – be prepared to give a lot of support with rhymes!

Checking Children's Learning
- Can children describe what a limerick is?

Revisiting the Objective
- Write a class version of Shared Writing Example 4.

Term 1 Unit of work 18:

Plan and continue the story

Writing Objective

T10: To write sustained stories using knowledge of story elements: narrative, settings, characterisation, dialogue and the language of story.

Links to Sentence/Word Level Work

S3: To use standard forms of verbs and to use the past tense consistently for narration.

Text Copymasters: C46–C47

Discussing the Text

- Explain that children are going to read the beginning of a story by a famous writer called Philippa Pearce.
- Read the extract 'What will happen next? Lion at school' on Resource Book pages 44 to 45.
- *What kind of story is this? Could it happen in real life?*
- *How does the little girl feel when the lion says he is going to eat her?*
- *How do you think she feels right at the end?*

Shared Writing

Session 1

Teacher Demonstration and Scribing

- Tell the children that they are going to write the story of what happened when the lion went to school. If the children already know this story, stress that they are going to compose their own version – written as if the lion was coming to your school.
- *First of all, I'm going to write some questions to help you think about and plan your stories. You'll need to have a name for the little girl, because that will make it easier to write the story.*
- Write the heading and first question of Shared Writing Example 1 (opposite). Ask for suggestions and scribe.
- Write the second question. Ask for suggestions and scribe, e.g. not really fierce, friendly, curious, clumsy.
- *Now this is a really important question because it will affect the whole of your story ...* Write question 3. Take children through some of the points to think about, e.g. If the answer were yes: *how would other children and the teachers feel about a lion appearing? Would it be hard to make anything funny happen?* If no: *would the little girl get blamed for anything the lion did eg eating up all her friends' school dinners?* Scribe these and other pros and cons the children or you can think of.
- Write the next question. *This is an important question too because what we write here will suggest some of the things that you could put into your story. I'll start you off ...* write: 'he might try and sit on the teacher's lap when she reads a story'.
- *Last of all we have to think about the end of the story.* Write the final question, take children's ideas and scribe.

Session 2

Supported Composition

- Read through the questions and notes from the previous session. Keep them on view throughout the time that children are writing their stories.

- *Today you are going to start writing your stories. To begin with, I want you to think about the first part of the story. I'm going to read you one way of opening the story. Listen carefully and then we'll decide if that is the sort of thing we want to write.*
- Read Shared Writing Example 2 (below). *What did you think of that? Was it a good way to start the story?*
- Ask children what you should write for your opening. Take suggestions and scribe.

Shared Writing Example

1. Planning questions

What could you call the little girl?

What is the lion really like?

Can other people see the lion?

What problems might there be in having the lion in school?

What will happen at the end of the school day?

2.

"Oh, all right!" said .... "You can come to school with me today but you have got to behave yourself. You are not allowed to eat anyone. Do you understand?"

The lion smiled a toothy smile. "Not even your teacher?" he asked.

Independent Writing

This should be spread over more than one session.

- The children should now write their stories. From time to time (or at the end of a session), review what children have written and then recap on what they might be writing in the next part.
- The children should read their work on completion and see if changes need to be made.

Checking Children's Learning

- How successfully have children used the planning questions and ideas?
- Did they find this helped them in their writing?
- Were they able to maintain consistency of person and tense?

Revisiting the Objective

- Plan a similar story where a boy meets a dragon and takes it to school.

Writing Objective

T12: To write simple evaluations of books giving reasons.

Links to Sentence/Word Level Work

S5: To write in clear sentences using capital letters and full stops accurately.

Text Copymasters: C48–C49

Discussing the Text

- Introduce the unit by telling children that they are going to write a review of a story. *A review of a book or a story tells other people who might not have read it what it is about. When you write a review you give your opinions of the book or the story ... you say what you thought about it and why. We are going to write a review of Little Red Riding Hood which we read earlier in this book. Let's read part of it again ...* If you have access to the full story from which the extract was taken, then you should read that with the children instead. The extract comes from the Pelican Big Book, *Little Red Riding Hood* by Stan Cullimore, published by Longman.
- Re-read pages 20 to 22 of the Resource Book. ('Little Red Riding Hood')
- Turn on to pages 46 and 47, 'Writing About A Book'. Go through the text, explaining to the children that the headings are designed to help them write the review.

Shared Writing

Session 1
Teacher Demonstration

- *When we are writing a review and we say what a story is about, we don't have to go into much detail – we just give an outline of the story. Let me show you ...*
- Using the acetate, write the Shared Writing Example, reading aloud and mentioning capital letters and punctuation as you write.

Shared Writing Example

In this book Stan Cullimore tells the story of Little Red Riding Hood and the wolf. The wolf pretends he is her granny so that he can eat Little Red Riding Hood. But Granny saves Little Red Riding Hood and the wolf runs away!

Teacher Scribing

- *Now we have to say what we think is the best part. Who can tell me which part they liked best? ... So, what shall I write down?* Adopting the majority opinion, take suggestions as to how it should be written and scribe. You may like to suggest including a quote from the text.
- Ask children's opinions of the illustrations. Get them to think about aspects such as whether or not they like them, how good they think they are, whether or not they are humorous, how the characters' appearance and feelings are shown, and use of colour. Discuss and then scribe the children's suggestions.
- Read back what has been written so far and tell children that you will complete the review tomorrow.

Session 2

Teacher Scribing

- Read what has been written so far and ask the children if they are happy with it or if there is anything they want to change.
- Take time out for children to discuss briefly in pairs what they think of the characters, e.g. do they seem real? Are they interesting? Which character do they like best? Ask children what they want you to write.

Supported Composition

- Discuss responses to the final question – especially the way the author writes and the use of rhyme to tell the story.
- Ask the children to write two sentences about the way the author writes.
- Share responses, select and scribe.
- Ask the children to write two sentences about what they think of the story.
- Share responses, select and scribe.

Independent Writing

- Give the children copies of Copymaster C3, 'Book Review'. Go through the reminders at the top. Children should then choose a book they have read recently and write a review of it.
- Display the reviews for other children to read.

Checking Children's Learning

- Can the children explain what a book review is and the sort of things it should include?
- Have the children covered all the reminder points in their writing?
- Have they written in clear sentences using capital letters and full stops accurately?

Revisiting the Objective

- Choose a text you have used recently in Shared Reading and write a class review.

Write a riddle

Writing Objective

T11: To invent own riddles, language puzzles, jokes.

Text Copymaster: C50

Discussing the Text

- Tell the children that they are going to read part of a poem which is like a riddle, and that you want them to guess what the poet is describing.
- Read the extract 'Riddle', which is from 'The Wind', by James Reeves (Resource Book page 48).
- *What is the poet describing?*
- Draw attention to the fact that the poet is talking about the wind as if it were a person.
- Discuss the number of lines, line length and rhyming pattern.

Shared Writing

Session 1
Teacher Demonstration

- Explain that you are going to write a riddle poem. You will write the first verse and you want the children to guess what you are describing. Explain that they must wait until you have finished writing before they tell you their guess.
- Write the first verse of the Shared Writing Example opposite. *Can you guess what my poem is about?*
- Read the poem. *Have I got the same pattern and shape to my poem as James Reeves had in his?*
- Write the first and second lines of the second verse leaving out 'sound'.

Teacher Scribing

- *I want us to finish this next verse together. What word could I put here which will tell readers how quiet snow is?*
- Complete the verse by getting children to supply the underlined parts in the Shared Writing Example, prompting and giving clues as necessary.
- Write the final verse in the same way.
- Read the poem together.

Session 2
Teacher Scribing

- Read the poem about snow again.
- Tell the children that they are going to write their own riddle poem about a storm, but this time they don't have to make it rhyme if they don't want to.
- Brainstorm and list (with good spacing) storm features, i.e. thunder, lightning, rain.

Supported Composition

- Ask the children to write down some words or phrases on their whiteboards which describe thunder – without using the word 'thunder'.
- Scribe suggestions – improving and adding if necessary, e.g. invisible, sounds like a lion roaring/a mountain tumbling down.
- Repeat for lightning and rain.

You can shape me or throw me,
    I'm cold to your touch,
It's no wonder that children
    enjoy me so much!

I can cover a garden
    and not make a <u>sound</u>,
I'm as soft as <u>a kitten</u>
    <u>when I'm on the ground</u>

You won't see me in Summer,
    just sometimes <u>in Spring,</u>
It's during the <u>Winter that</u>
    <u>I change everything!</u>

Independent Writing
- Children should use the scribed suggestions to write a three-verse riddle poem about a storm.
- Share poems with the group or class.

Checking Children's Learning
- Have children written in the first person?
- Have they managed to avoid naming the subject of the poem?

Revisiting the Objective
- Write a riddle poem together about a more unusual animal such as an elephant, camel or giraffe.

Look – Say – Fold – Write – Check

Word	First try	Second try	Third try
could			
would			
because			

Planning a Story

Who is the main character in the story?	
Who else is in the story?	
Where does it take place?	
How does it begin?	
What happens next?	
What happens then?	
How does it end?	
A title for the story	

When you write a book review you should say

- what the story is about
- what you think is the best part
- what you think of the story and the way the author writes.

- what you think of the characters
- what you think of the illustrations

Title of the book:

Author: **Illustrator:**

Publisher: **Reviewed by:**

Money Doesn't Grow On Trees

My mum took me shopping last Saturday. I HATE SHOPPING!

"I know you hate going shopping," she said, "but you'll just have to put up with it because you need some new shoes for school."

It was sunny. I could have been out playing football ... but no, I had to go shopping. I could have gone round to my friend Jake's house next door ... but no, I had to go shopping.

Units of work 1 and 2

We got on the bus (I was moaning).
We got to the shopping centre (I was
still moaning).

"I'm going to get really cross if you
don't stop moaning and groaning!"
Mum said. I decided I'd better be quiet.
When my mum gets cross she
REALLY gets cross!

Units of work 1 and 2

When we got to the shoe shop I cheered up. I saw some brilliant trainers that would have been just right for school.

"Can I have those, please Mum?" I asked her.

She looked at me and I could see what the answer was going to be from the look on her face.

"No, you can't," she said. "You need some proper school shoes for the winter. I'm sorry, love, but you can't have trainers as well as shoes. I'm not made of money, you know."

Units of work 1 and 2

I did know. She was always saying that. No that's not true – sometimes she says, "Money doesn't grow on trees, you know!" I wish it did!

We went to look at what my mum calls proper school shoes. I didn't like the first pair that I tried on but the second ones were OK. My friend Jake had some the same but I didn't want to tell Mum that.

Units of work 1 and 2

"Well then? Do you like them?" Mum asked.

"They're not as good as the trainers ... but they're OK," I said.

Mum went off to pay for my new shoes while I waited by the door. I wondered if it was worth asking Mum if we could have an ice-cream before we went home. I wondered which she would say ... would it be "I'm not made of money, you know." or "Money doesn't grow on trees, you know!"

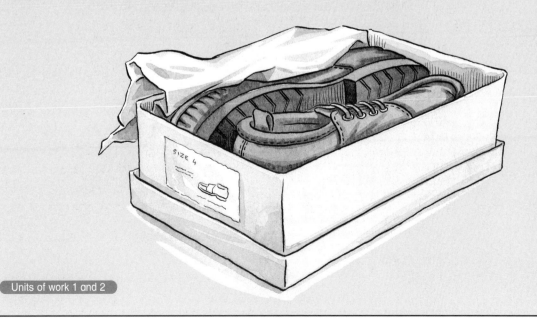

As we were walking past the ice-cream van I asked her. She looked at me and then she laughed, "I know I'm not made of money but I think I can manage two ice-creams!"

Wendy Body

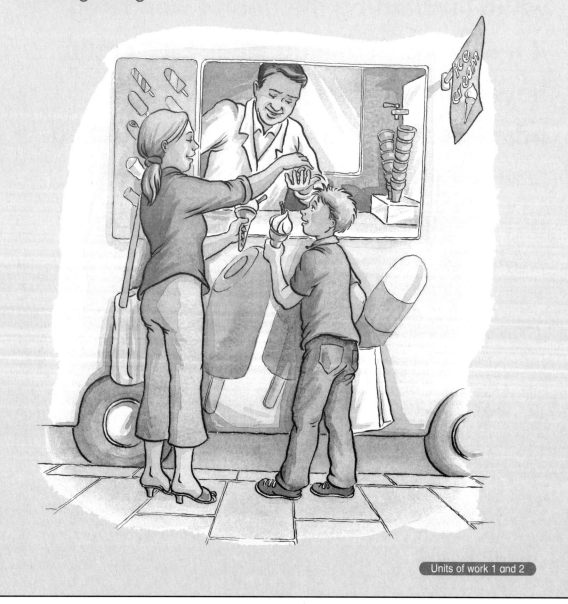

Jonah's Den

1

2

3

4

Units of work 3 and 4

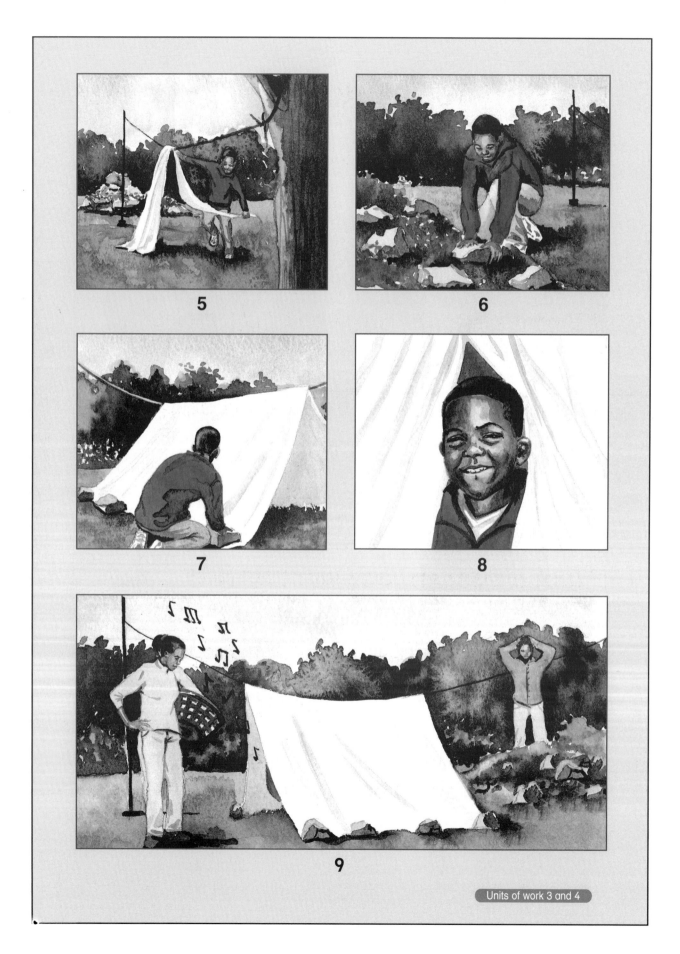

Five fat sausages

Five fat sausages frying in a pan,
All of a sudden, one went BANG!

Four fat sausages frying in a pan,
All of a sudden, one went BANG!

Three fat sausages frying in a pan,
All of a sudden, one went BANG!

Two fat sausages frying in a pan,
All of a sudden, one went BANG!

One fat sausage frying in a pan,
All of a sudden, one went BANG!

There were no fat sausages frying
in the pan!

Unit of work 5

Fishes in the sea!

One, two, three, fishes in the sea.

Four, five, six, mermaids doing tricks!

Unit of work 6

Seven, eight, nine, lobsters in a line.

Here comes another lobster, that makes ten,
and three little fishes want to watch it all again!

Little Red Riding Hood

This is the story of a _____ girl

who ____ always as good as gold.

Her name _____ Little Red Riding Hood

and she was only six years _____.

Unit of work 7

One day her mum _____ a brambly pie –

with a sweet and brambly _____!

"_____ this to Gran," said Mum to the girl,

"Your Granny is not feeling _____."

Unit of work 7

So the good little _____ picked up the pie

and _____ on her red riding hood.

Then _____ she went to her

Granny's _____

which was hidden _____ in a wood.

Unit of work 7

But as she happily _____ through the trees,

somebody watched her go _____ ...

A naughty wolf, _____ a hungry tummy

had a naughty _____ in his eye!

Unit of work 7

That _____ wolf, he looked at the

_____

wearing her red riding _____.

He _____ his lips and he rubbed his

tummy –

and said, "I'd eat *her* if I _____!"

So he ran _____ the trees to

Granny's _____

where he _____, "Quick, let me in!"

But _____ Granny opened her little

front _____,

He popped her straight in the _____!

Unit of work 7

She went through the house
  to Granny's room
and saw someone lying in bed.
But it didn't look quite like her Granny –
and so the little girl said,

"Oh, Granny – what hairy hands you
  have."
To which the Wolf replied ...
"I know my hands are hairy, my child.
But come in and sit by my side."

Unit of work 8

"Oh, Granny – what beady eyes you
have."
The Wolf, he smiled and said …
"My eyes are beady but I'm getting
quite old.
Come closer and sit by my bed."

Unit of work 8

"Oh, Granny – what pointy teeth you
　　have."
The Wolf, he got *mad* as can be …
"Just come here at once, you *stupid*
　　child!
I'm hungry and *you* are my tea!"

Stan Cullimore

Unit of work 8

A Character Portrait of the Wolf

What we can tell from the text:

What we can tell from the illustrations:

Unit of work 8

A Magical Cave

Soon, with the sound of crashing waves and the sad cries of seagulls all around them, they reached the entrance to a cave. Estelle had been there before so she knew that it was a dark, damp and gloomy place. She was very surprised therefore when she saw a soft glow of light coming from inside.

As she went into the cave, Estelle gasped in amazement. The dark granite walls she had seen before had gone. The hidden pools and clumps of slippery seaweed had disappeared as well.

Units of work 9 and 10

Units of work 9 and 10

Now the walls were sparkling in the soft glowing light as if they were studded with a thousand jewels. Smooth golden sand spread out on each side of a silver path and strange but beautiful flowers waved gently as she brushed past them with her skirt.

On they went through the magical cave until they reached a large heavy door. The man unlocked it and Estelle followed him as he pulled open the door and went through.

Wendy Body

Units of work 9 and 10

The Inside–Outside Man

I'm the back to front and all mixed up,
inside–outside man,
with an inside–outside, under and over,
backwards and forwards van.

I wear my trousers up to my knees,
my socks go on over my boots,
my shirts are always back to front
and it's inside out for my suits.

My van, which I call Matilda,
is painted in yellow and black,
Matilda is slow going forwards,
but terribly fast coming back!

Units of work 11 to 13

I live in a special mixed-up house
where I go downstairs to bed,
the bed's too short and I'm too tall
so I sleep standing up on my head.

The kitchen's upstairs in the attic,
the bathroom is by the front door,
there are carpets above on my ceilings,
and the lights are below on the floor.

The TV's outside in the garden,
the pond is inside in the hall –
the garden might be a big one
but the pond is really too small.

Yes I'm back to front and all mixed up,
I'm the inside–outside man,
with an inside–outside, under and over,
backwards and forwards van.

Wendy Body

Units of work 11 to 13

Strange Bumps

Owl was in bed.

"It is time to blow out the candle and go to sleep," he said with a yawn.

Then owl saw two bumps under the blanket at the bottom of his bed.

"What can those strange bumps be?" asked Owl.

Unit of work 14

Owl lifted up the blanket. He looked down into the bed. All he could see was darkness. Owl tried to sleep, but he could not.

"What if those two strange bumps grow bigger and bigger while I am asleep?" said Owl. That would not be pleasant. Owl moved his right foot up and down. The bump on the right moved up and down.

Unit of work 14

Pelican Shared Writing Fiction Teacher's Book Year 2 © Pearson Education Limited 2001

"One of those bumps is moving!" said Owl.

Owl moved his left foot up and down. The bump on the left moved up and down.

"The other bump is moving!" cried Owl.

Owl pulled all of the covers off his bed. The bumps had gone. All Owl could see at the bottom of his bed were his own two feet.

"But now I am cold," said Owl. "I will cover myself with the blankets again."

As soon as he did, he saw the same two bumps.

"Those bumps are back!" shouted Owl.

Pelican Shared Writing Fiction Teacher's Book Year 2 © Pearson Education Limited 2001

Unit of work 14

"Bumps, bumps, bumps! I will never sleep tonight!"

Owl jumped up and down on top of his bed.

"Where are you? What are you?" he cried. With a crash and a bang the bed came falling down.

Owl ran to the top of the stairs. He sat in his chair near the fire.

"I will let those two strange bumps sit on my bed all by themselves," said Owl. "Let them grow as big as they wish. I will sleep right here where I am safe."

And that is what he did.

Arnold Lobel

Unit of work 14

Writing Tongue Twisters!

Two tired tigers and a tortoise take tea
as six silly seals sail slowly on the sea.

Unit of work 15

Five flying fairies fall flat on their faces round rushing red robots all running races.

Unit of work 15

Planning a Story

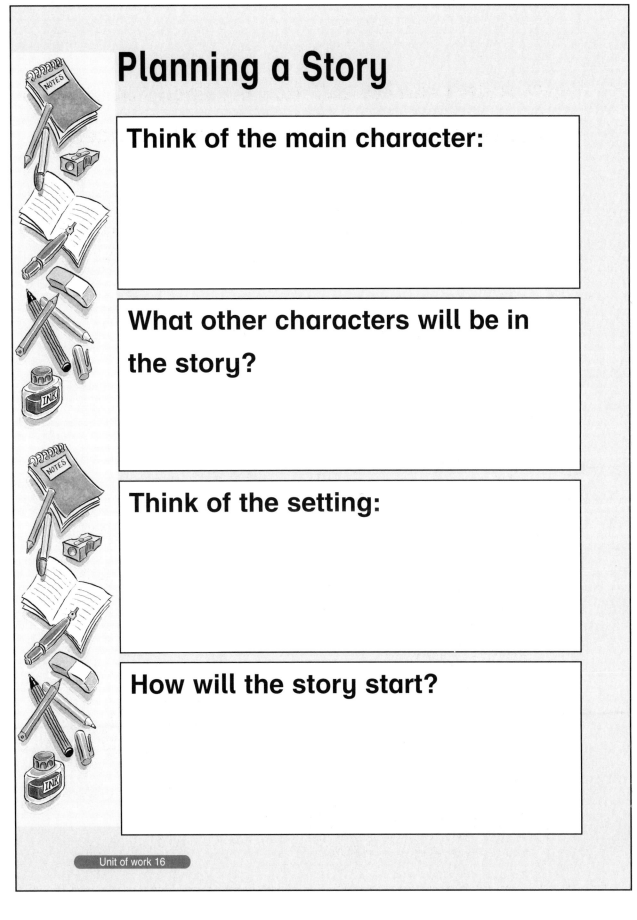

Think of the main character:

What other characters will be in the story?

Think of the setting:

How will the story start?

Unit of work 16

What will happen in the middle?

What will happen at the end?

What could you call your story?

Two Funny Limericks

There was a young farmer of Leeds

Who swallowed six packets of seeds,

It soon came to pass

He was covered with grass,

And he couldn't sit down for the weeds.

Anon

Unit of work 17

There was an old man with a beard,
Who said, "it is just as I feared! -
Two Owls and a Hen,
Four Larks and a Wren,
Have all built their nest in my beard!"

Edward Lear

Unit of work 17

What will happen next?

Lion at school

Once upon a time there was a little girl who didn't like going to school. She always set off late. Then she had to hurry, but she never hurried fast enough.

One morning she was hurrying along as usual when she turned a corner and there stood a lion, blocking her way. He stood waiting for her. He stared at her with his yellow eyes. He growled, and when he growled the little girl could see that his teeth were as sharp as skewers and knives. He growled: "I'm going to eat you up."

Pelican Shared Writing Fiction Teacher's Book Year 2 © Pearson Education Limited 2001

"Oh dear!" said the little girl, and she began to cry.

"Wait!" said the lion. "I haven't finished. I'm going to eat you up UNLESS you take me to school with you." ...

Philippa Pearce

Unit of work 18

Writing About A Book

Title of the book: Little Red Riding Hood

The author: Stan Cullimore

The illustrator: Denise Elliott

The publisher: Longman

What is the story about?

Which do you think is the best part?

What do you think of the illustrations?

Unit of work 19

What do you think of the characters?

What do you think of the story and the way the author writes?

Unit of work 19

Riddle

I can get through a doorway

without any key,

And strip the leaves

from the great oak tree.

James Reeves

Unit of work 20